Tales from...

BEHIND THE FITTING ROOM CURTAIN

by

Molly Hanger

First published in Great Britain as a softback original in 2014

Copyright © 2014 Molly Hanger

The moral right of this author has been asserted.

Typeset in Century Schoolbook

Editing, design and publishing by UK Book Publishing

UK Book Publishing is a trading name of Consilience Media

www.ukbookpublishing.com

ISBN: 978-1-910223-24-6

Contents

Foreword

Dedicated to every sales person who has graced the shop floor in retail. I salute you for your endurance in a field of work where there is little thanks for the service we provide. For those of you who have ever wondered why we enter this world of high drama for low pay on a daily basis to be at your beck and call, be entertained by how we view you, the customer, and marvel at the skills we have developed over time which allow you to enter into our world on the shop floor, to the time you leave with your purchase clasped in hand.

My Why

Why did I enter this crazy world of Retail as a career? Ask that question of everything you do in life. There is always a "Why" and a definitive moment in time.

In my case, my why happened in Los Angeles in the summer of 2008. I was sat alone outside in the evening, a beautiful skyline, warm with a breeze that danced around along with the chatter and laughter of surrounding tables. There I was pondering the flight times of the following day and the routine I was going back to and no amount of rye and dry was going to alter that or mask the mountain of washing I faced on touchdown at Heathrow.

Jennifer, my daughter, had sailed through prep school, and as a mother I had become redundant, as we all do when they become a full time student at such a tender age, discovering her new world of school life. Like it or not my services as a mother were no longer required during daytime hours between 8 and 4. I had taken the option of staying at home to be a full time mother, walked away from a career and found myself with time to spare. Desperate now to flee the routine of housework and morning breaks which consisted of tuning in to daytime television only to be met with the latest

1

recipe that can be done as quick as the presenter (well in their world! Reality is slightly different as we all know when you only have one oven and one pair of hands and not 'one I prepared earlier just in case') or better still coffee in hand peruse the morning paper to stare in amazement as to what diet is going to shift the excess being pregnant leaves behind – but never mind, girls, turn the page and the latest craze in magic knickers will hide it all for you, even if it does push it up and out somewhere else! Saints preserve us was this really it? I had lost that 9-5 routine six years ago and I missed it. The problem now as I twizzled the ice round the glass for the umpteenth time was what would fit around school hours?

I never thought about retail, unless of course I was shopping and I had a degree in that earned over so many years – in fact I had a bloody Distinction as my then husband and credit card could testify to! After multi-tasking as a mother for six years it wouldn't be that bad or hard and I would get back that independence and my own money, more to the point. Sales girls always seemed to possess that certain confidence and smile to boot. If I could tackle the world of Insurance for 23 years then surely retail would be a walk in the park? Little did I know at this point the demands of the shop floor and the skills necessary to open and close a sale with a sales pitch to a customer a cabinet minister would be proud of, not to mention re-education of footwear in heels I haven't worn since junior school but would become, in the early days, your new best friend.

On my return to our hotel room I announced to the other half that I would be getting a job on my return home. That statement and certain voice we all ladies have didn't prompt a response, just a bewildered look, no words and my decision was made there and then. And this is where my story really begins and my collection of experiences unfolds to you, the reader.

Cutting my teeth in the Department Store

Once I had completed the jobs women hate on return from holiday, I set about finding a job in retail. I had always felt at ease in one particular department store and was determined after hearing they had vacancies coming up. CV in hand, I took myself into town dressed in black and white to look the part. There would no longer be a part to play for a business suit in the future, nor killer heels come to think of it – those went out of the window in my second trimester of pregnancy and only had a brief airing on nights out – but they do make an appearance later on with nasty repercussions!

I had a call a few weeks later to attend an interview for a sales assistant's job for a new concession which would open up in time for the run up to Christmas. Would I come in for an interview with the owner of the Company? Would I be interested? You try stopping me! I was already deducting staff discount in my head for the cosmetics hall and was halfway up the escalator to fashion on the first floor for the dress I had seen before the holiday.

The day of the interview arrived and I sat reading a paper, waiting my turn to be seen. The last time that happened was years ago. I wasn't nervous,

4

quite excited really at the prospect of a decent conversation that didn't involve Shaun the Sheep or this week's shopping list at the supermarket. The owner of the company was not a lady to be messed with, but she liked the fact that I was straight to the point with her as far as my little one was concerned and I had to fit this around school hours and school holidays. I had the skills she was looking for, a natural way with people, presentable with a good sense of humour and strong liaising skills. Trust me: after 20 years of dealing with farmers in the Insurance industry I had this one in the bag. I would be working with a girl some years younger than me, and subject to her approval the job was mine. I was back in the land of the living, contracted to four hours a day including Saturdays, over the service window, which to anyone not connected to retail means lunchtime 11-3 and this was perfect. Next was to meet my immediate line manager.

The day I met Adie was one I will not forget. It always makes me smile when youth has a standard view on what a typical 48 year old should look like and she had been landed with me and was dreading it. To coin her phrase at the time "And in you walked" – not the picture she had imagined – and we hit it off straightaway over a coffee. The following month we would be working together, in Jewellery, and I had homework to do.

Arriving at the store on my first day I was shown the locker room where over the coming 18 months would see clouds of hairspray (usually mine) and see the laughter and tears of life on the shop floor. Branded store badge pinned on to my shirt, I took my first walk onto the shop floor. Gone is the fixed smile reserved for the customer, you are now one of the girls and woe betide any customer who thinks they have the upper hand. There are ways and means to deal with said customer without a word being uttered and if you play it right you can melt the heart of any tiger and turn them into a pussycat. It is a skill that comes with time, experience and the patience of a saint, but it works and is an art you must learn if you are to survive. The customer is the customer and is always right? I smile now at that one and shall not give my answer.

I look back on those early days often and recall the steep learning curve and lessons learned over time. Truth be known they usually come to mind when I see a new member of staff walk onto the floor for the first time and sense the nervous walk and other body language signs that give them away as new to the world of retail to customers as they browse the latest trends with a question or two, only for the new lamb to the slaughter to announce that she is new and apologises profusely as she doesn't know the answer. Oh, my dear, you will learn quickly and will think nothing of this line of questioning and what goes with the territory in the world of retail six months from now.

For four short hours a day I had my independence back and my confidence returned. I was no longer just the Mother, the Wife – I was the girl I used to be and loving every minute of it. My feet had other ideas though, but adapted well to carefully chosen Clarks shoes as support to cushion the hammering they took on the shop floor. There was and still is the coldness of the kitchen floor when I return home, kick off my shoes and enjoy that 'Ah' moment I am sure many of you readers connected to this industry can relate to.

Sales are easy to achieve over the phone, and any other issues to boot, come to think of it. Selling on the floor is a completely different kettle of fish though as the customer being visible demanded new skills of reading facial and body language signals, not to mention conversation and rapport techniques. Adie was a great teacher and we became a strong team – the 'Dream Team' – as we quickly built our customer base with a range of products not available to many stores outside of London at the time, coupled with the merchandising skills of a four-four-two formation that delivered results any Premier Football Manager would be proud of. We were on a high. Christmas now beckoned.

All that is Christmas!

How far I had come in those few short months
leading up to Christmas. At this point I am going
to generalise on the festive season as I cover so
many years and several brands in the process, so
to you, the reader, what comes next pretty much
sums it up for me. I don't need to tell you or insult
your intelligence as to when the festive season is
upon us. At one time, if childhood memory serves
me well, Christmas cards, baubles with tinsel for
good measure, rarely made an appearance until the
last sparkler fizzled out on Bonfire Night. Nowadays
it begins in August before the children return to
school, and the cards to tempt us are usually the
remnants of last year's stock at a crazy offer to rid
the stockroom in preparation for this year's must-
have glittered reindeer collection. Easter begins on
Boxing Day just as a reminder in case you want to
stock up on your creme eggs! Lord, I could let rip
like so many of you on the commercialism of it all,
despite the fact I work in retail, but will be a good
girl on this occasion.

Whilst you are all layering on the sun block the
stockrooms will be getting fat with deliveries of all
shapes and sizes and staff will be hanging upside
down like fruit bats finding a place for the boxes
and packaging that wipes out an entire rainforest to
ensure every customer is tempted by the must-have

gadget, decoration, chocolate and novelty sock that would put Santa's grotto to shame. And so begins the quarter all retailers know will make or break them come New Year. Get the product right, whether it be any of the above not to mention the 'dress' to knock the competition off the dance floor at the annual office bash or suffer the consequences and beg for mercy from the customer in the New Year sales.

The one customer every retail assistant will covet is the male, for he usually appears out of hibernation early December with a shopping list given by the female species, and come Christmas Eve will be out in force. Desperation is the look which, from a woman's point of view on the floor, is easy to recognise and capitalise on, especially when the humble Christmas lunch is at stake. It is make or break and the solution is in our hands. "Size, Sir?" which will prompt the startled rabbit stare." Colour" and" Occasion"? And don't even get me started on Lingerie. A quiet whisper reminds the male that before leaving the nest with list a peek in the wardrobe at the size label is the order of the day. A look up and down at several girls on the shop floor, squaring up the hip, bust, height and a pair of shapely legs will not resolve this one, no matter how hard we try, but the extended returns policy into the second week of January may well be his only salvation come Christmas morning. Gift wrap service? Please do not push your luck I have thought many a time – a store bag and tissue is as far as it gets at 4pm, Christmas Eve.

Turning to you, ladies, you may well look at us with contempt as you ignore our "Good Mornings" on meet and greet, but come the fitting room are more than happy to get all the advice you can get, not only on the dress you have tried on but the accessories to finish, not to mention the brand of all-in-one tights to be worn to avoid the dreaded VPL.

For the entire month of December retail staff will be surrounded by all that is Christmas, and have been tortured by the same music – and believe me on the fourth round in the hours of service window lost the will to live as Bing Crosby's White Christmas echoes once more. "Do you ever get fed up with the music?" – I got asked that question once. "Fed up?" – Oh yes! that usually registers last week of November by which time we all know the playlist of the CD from back to front, and we are stuck with it well into January Sales as someone at Head Office usually forgets to change it to the upbeat, non-seasonal we are more familiar with all year round, and that never changes either, come to think of it!

Late night shopping can be brisk once office workers leave and pop in on their way home as they now have that extra four hours to play with. Shops, whether large or small, stay open with the favourite late night designated as Thursday. Year in and out this is the night retail management think you will abandon tea and stay in town, on the last four Thursdays of the month leading up to Christmas. Truth of the matter is that after a long day you will manage an hour or two at the very latest, and come 7pm the only life to be seen in the city centre are people dressed up to the nines on their way to Christmas parties. However, fear not, as closing time approaches you can guarantee – and staff will have bets on this – five minutes before closing a customer will land on the floor. The fact that it is the only customer in the whole of the last two hours has nothing to do with it. Keys jangling louder that jingle bells are a sure enough hint that their time is up and with aching feet and Christmas lights to guide you home we will repeat the same performance for the remaining three Thursdays. The powers-that-be may be convinced that this particular evening is the only free time for the consumer to shop. The fact that they already started in the January sales and finished at the end of August sales event will not convince them otherwise, and so the tradition remains, as much set in stone as the lighting of the Blue Peter Advent candle.

Internet shopping rules the roost on this one as time is limited to browse along with family commitments at this time of year. The offer of a mince pie whilst you shop till you drop will not tempt you away from your sofa as the build-up to the Christmas soap cliff-hanger draws ever closer. Christmas Eve at close of business will herald the one day off in retail. Whatever happened to "If you didn't have it by Christmas Eve that was it until 2nd January!"? How times have changed as childhood memories come flooding back as I stuff the turkey with one hand and enjoy a well earned Baileys over ice with the other. I wish I could bottle the constant "Merry Christmases" and warm smiles customers freely and heartily say to us all who work the long hours to make your Christmas complete, some of you with a swagger as you stopped for a commercial break in the local, half way through your shopping expedition. lt is the rare time the customer and retail staff will agree on anything.

Batten down the hatches, we're in Sale

Is there such a thing these days, as it appears to be a permanent state of affairs on the high street? At one time two annual sales had real impact on the high street – New Year and Summer. Nowadays, we have Mid-Season, Bank Holiday events, promotions on new collections to herald Autumn/Winter, Spring and Summer and the list goes on. The recession has re-educated the consumer into a savvy shopper and the high street has paid the price – shot itself in the foot in the process, so to speak, to ensure footfall remains constant. Emails remind you, the customer, days before sales/promotions commence – but we don't really have to do that for regulars to stores and brands have a diary of your own. You know better than the staff when events and sales are due and often remind us with a smile broader than a Cheshire cat coupled with the classic line of "I will leave it till the end of the week as you will be in Sale"!

Swing tickets out in colours you all recognise and scanners and printers charged and loaded – there is anticipation for you and high activity on the shop floor for staff. Whilst sales assistants are on the shop floor, the sales shopper is hovering behind them. There is a look between sales assistant and shopper.

You know that the little black number she has been eyeing up for the last two months is now within her budget and she knows you know this fact by your smile. "Just browsing" is all that will be said. "Just browsing my foot!" It will not matter if there is six foot of snow tomorrow morning. One thing is for certain: she will be back through your door at 9am faster than a ferret up a drainpipe for said dress and will be over to you at the till point gushing the words "Such a bargain"! No need to try on coveted dress – it's already been in and out of the fitting room half a dozen times with the "I'm just not sure it's me" routine, together with the fact she knows the returns policy on sale items better than any member of staff. She will then return to the office and her purchase will be the topic of conversation for the remainder of the day. Once home, the prize will be in the wardrobe. At some point in the future, whether it be immediate for that special date or family gathering, it will be worn and the familiar tone of voice from the other half will utter the famous line all women dread "New dress?". The reply, already rehearsed from years of practice: "Shows how much notice you take, I've had it for ages!" is said in the same tone back. Any man who values his life will go back to reading his paper and let sleeping dogs lie on this one.

Promotional and Mid-Season Sales are a delight to work and regular customers whom staff have come

to know and chat to on a regular basis will buy
from new season collections to add to existing pieces
in their already bulging wardrobes, from seasons
gone by. We treasure them and probably know more
about their lives than their family members do.
Internet shopping can save you time to some degree
in your busy world, but I do think nothing beats
letting off steam of how little Johnny's antics this
morning caused you to miss out on the parking slot
you rely on. It all adds to your shopping experience
as you wave us goodbye, happy with your 40%
off. No amount of technology can beat the human
interaction on the high street.

The end of Main Sale events invite a rather
different customer onto the shop floor – not the
regular customers we are used to. "Oh no!" The
hardened 'I am going to shop when the price is
right', disrespectful one will land on the floor. By
this time the swing tickets are frayed due to the
constant to-ing and fro-ing to the fitting room and
shopgirls are at their wits' end searching for stock
on computer systems nationwide, as you left it to the
final week in the hope that further markdowns are
applied, before you shop the rails, only to find after
eight weeks of sale only size 8s and 20s are left. Your
attitude will be one of dismay that the size 12 top
you have had your eye on for the last three months
is now out of stock and someone is going to get it in
the neck. As you huff and puff yourself along the

rails of sorry alternatives, suitcase now down one item and you leave for Greece on Saturday, hangers will fly off the rails or fall off mid rail onto the floor underneath – and will you pick up fallen clothing? Not likely! Unless the corner of your eye meets that of the sales assistant whose eye contact back to you will rebuke you and suggest you pick it up. No words need to be spoken: the 'look' says it all. Fallen items will be picked up and placed on top of the rail before you depart with the face of thunder and speed any marathon walker would be proud of.

If you think it stops there, you are mistaken. Final weeks of sale bring into play further reductions and hard sale markdowns. Now, you may think we know when all this is going to happen – the fact we only found out via comms on the morning brief has nothing to do with it. A further discount has now been applied and as sod's law dictates it is the day after you made your purchase and it would have been all the sweeter with an additional 10% off. This brings out the animal in you and we brace ourselves for the flack that is coming. Returns policy on sale items comes into play and it is hangers at ten paces. Items are returned, labels still in place, naturally. You will return tomorrow and buy back with the extra 10% off! A triumphant smirk will remind staff who has the upper hand on this one, and I will remind myself to add a glass of red to tonight's evening meal. Don't you just love Sales!

Competition will be rife between brands in sale periods. Windows will be changed with gusto on a weekly basis; sale banners too, for that matter, just to remind you of the ever increasing percentages off. Limited additional percentages guaranteed on final sale weekends just to tempt you more, and if one does it all the rest will follow suit or go one step further with the bogoff (buy one get one for free) or bogohf (buy one get one half price) on higher valued stock. Last day of sale will be the most frantic and close of business will bring relief to staff, joy to the customer and well earned profit to the brand if both weather and customer have stayed loyal.

Scanners, printers, sales guns, swing tickets, window banners and A4 posters displayed for weeks on end are removed and packed away. Guess what? –transition collections for New Season collections arrive next week and yes you have it! There will be a promotion on Outerwear with a Mystery Shopper on the loose.

'The Mystery Shopper'

Is it me or have we become a nation obsessed with customer feedback to the point of ridicule? Let's look at some prime examples from everyday activities we all do and you will see exactly where I am coming from. I am a busy working mother. I drop off my little one at school and then concentrate on my day ahead, and part of that comes with a cup of Americano coffee at my favourite coffee house en route. This is part of my daily routine and I will sit and read the papers, watch the world go by and calm down after World War 3 has virtually been declared getting my little one up and both of us off on time for the school run, then we will kiss and make up from the drama around 7am, as we walk into school. You all know the routine. It goes without saying that a text will be sent from Customer services asking how I rated my cup of coffee – not one question, of course, but a whole list ranging from cleanliness to a member of staff I found who had gone the extra mile in service and could I think of anything that would enhance my experience? Give me strength! A cup of coffee, a catch up with the regulars and staff I have come to know, whether it be a nod or five minutes putting the world to rights is all I need, and if I didn't enjoy that – and more to the point the coffee – would I still have a loyalty card and sit at my favourite table? However, there is always a little carrot dangling of 'entry to a draw' as they put it, so you are either going to complete or delete the little text – the choice is yours on this one.

After delivery of my weekly shop, the online supermarket of the year will, the morning after, without fail, send me a text asking me how satisfied I was with the service my supermarket delivery driver provided during my latest delivery and 'could I rate between 1 and 10?'! Well that is an easy one: he arrived at the back door with boxes from the van, I took out the shopping from the boxes, signed for it and he left. If there is anything else to say that one is between me and customer services – the delivery man isn't the problem; the fact that they omitted one item that kicked the recipe for the meal I was cooking for Sunday dinner, without telling me via text is, however, so what the driver has got to do with it lord knows! But I still shop with them because usually they get it right and it fits in with my lifestyle.

Next, and this is the same day and start of the week – oh by the way it is Monday morning I might add – the Summer club where my daughter attends over the holidays: hope all is well with my camp experience and if there is anything more they can do to help please can I talk to the camp manager on the number provided!-I only dropped her off at 8am and the text was sent at 12.30! The fact she enjoys going and this is her third summer should speak volumes as to why I put my trust in them. Do they really need me to say anymore? And if there are any issues would I not tell the camp manager at 8am, when I signed her in!

The list goes on and it seems that Big Brother out there wants to know every little detail and is in a way the invisible Mystery Shopper. What happens on the floor is totally different as little Mystery Shopper has two arms and legs, is not sent via text and is now on the loose. Now, let's get back to the two words that will put the fear of god into a retail assistant and make the hair on the back of her neck stand up. A morning brief will announce the return of the Mystery shopper just to make you aware of it. At this point the last result will be brought up. A good report puts you in the green zone and it is 'well done' and sighs of relief all round. Get a bad one and land in the red zone: little Mystery Shopper will be back out within the month to ensure that the hauling over the coals, tantamount to a court martial for the poor staff member involved, has been enough to rectify the error of your ways and you are in compliance with set procedures. The fact that little Mystery Shopper landed on the one day you were a staff member down, will give their opinion based on their visit, a snapshot in time on how they feel service has been given to them and would like to think is the benchmark for all customers that follow, no matter what the circumstances on the floor might be – and it goes something like this:

On arrival were you greeted within a set number
of minutes? And trust me it isn't long. A good retail
assistant will pick up on everyone and work the floor
to ensure that you are welcomed. Were you asked
effective questions with suitable products suggested?
Now come on, ladies, how many of you are greeted
for you to just walk past us without even a response?
And as far as products to be suggested: look at us
with fair warning that if we utter one more word of
assistance the "I am just browsing" comes into play
– or better still you moved like greased lightning to
the next collection on the opposite side of the room. I
had one lady who snapped "I want to be left alone"! –
Fine, I will leave you and Marlene Dietrich to it then.

Having passed the first two stages and taken into
consideration the occasion, colours you like to wear,
body type and nothing that is not knee length will
suffice, a top is now the order of the day. We do our
best to offer suggestions on our way to fitting, with
accessories to complete the look. Upon entering the
fitting room, we will invite you to come out, once
ready, to check the fit and suggest more alternatives
or ways to customise with your existing wardrobe.
We advise you of current promotions, as we did on
greeting you and introduce the benefits of opening
a store card with us, especially as it entitles you to
a discount on all your purchases in one transaction
that day. Major brownie points if the Mystery
Shopper notes this one down on the report!

After all the service given, the crunch now is are/ were you encouraged to buy, which is always a tricky one and the words hard sell could easily slip in – and the name of the retail assistant, as the name on the badge is clearly visible. Many of you will not buy and will utter words already familiar to the fitting room assistant, who has catered to your every need and brought in further items from the shop floor; we know the classic word or phrase that you will use. Finally, was the farewell up to standard as you left? As you tot up your score from the minute you arrived, looking at your watch, having eyed and scrutinised the floor and all staff with a performance that would have given you the part for the role of Poirot... we wait with bated breath for the report to land.

In the meantime over a two week period there will be several times when eye contact between staff and certain questions asked from a customer on the floor indicate the likelihood of a Mystery Shopper or one that has just left – and bloody hell, you or someone else forgot about one of the key elements. But hey, it was only Bank Holiday Saturday and one of our key sales weekends of the year. Like everything else to do with surveys, let's remember one thing: there is a famous saying "If it isn't broken don't fix it". Your customer base and profit margins speak louder than any Mystery Shopper.

Delivery and the four words I am renowned for!

Mystery shopper results and the stress and strain of main sale events now give way to the excitement of new season. Mondays and Wednesdays each week – or every day in some cases – whether it be accompanied by the glow of early morning sunrise or pitch black and a chill in the air – a fleet of lorries each bearing every brand name under the sun will choke the high street. Pallets and rails hiding the identity of precious stock, already given press coverage months ago of what will be the key look of the season ahead, are whisked inside. This will be the routine for the months to come and retailers are glad of it. Tired stock and sales rails are replaced by new fashions' drop capsules, emailed out under training modules, which are digested by staff weeks before and whet their appetites, but sadly so many times do not reflect the look and feel of the actual garment in all its glory until delivered. Whether it sells or seals the fate of a collection or a complete season is another story.

I love the freshness transition collections bring with them and how they transform the floor. The girls know me so well that on seeing me eyeing the stock, they know at some point the four words I am renowned for will come into play each delivery day, and they will be revealed to you later. On arrival, they are unpackaged from layers of plastic and are now waiting for scrutiny by staff, who will take on board the collection name and story behind the look, already rehearsed since the fashion drop email. Now to be delivered to an eager audience, to you, the customer, with a pitch on colour, cut and style to ensure each piece is the must-have your wardrobe cannot be without, and is sold. Any element of doubt is cast to one side by the mannequins in the windows, dressed to perfection, and staff, who, by way of uniform choices, grace the floor better than any show ring at the Grand National on Ladies' Day. Both of these marketing techniques more or less guarantee the sight of your hard earned cash or the ever flexible plastic friend as you coo with delight the minute your pin number is accepted and you now have the 'to-die-for' item to turn other mothers green with envy at the school gates come Monday morning. Clever staff have other means of persuasion, as they model the new look of the season on their way into work, passing you on their daily walk. You will give them a side glance and the unspoken "I'm having that this winter" look is given back, which we are all accustomed to! We really are clever, underestimated sales mannequins as we weave in and out amongst you during rush hour foot traffic.

Putting together a 'look' is a challenge I relish as do other stylists on the floor. It is an enviable quality to have, part of her own personality that is taken for granted yet the power of it can be an intoxicating drug. It is a skill learned over so many years and becomes her trade mark in this industry, as mine is now. We each of us customise pieces to suit our personality, size and style. Simple and easy. It is what sells the collection or any product in this business so never underestimate us.

There is, however, always a piece in a collection that will never, no matter what or how it is promoted by staff, signage or the fashion press, be accepted by the customer, irrespective of discounts or at the very last resort sidelined to hard markdown sale, be sold. It is the piece quickly identified on arrival and labelled with the four words I am renowned for. The girls on the floor wait and expect me to say, as they know my style and the expression to expect on standing before them, and the raising of four fingers on my right hand as I deliver the words "see you in sale", the tone of voice echoing the disbelief of the buyer's choice on this one. After several minutes of laughter follows the line "We knew you would say it". Let's not go there, as we resign ourselves to the fact there is another one to add to the rail of fame in the stockroom. It will still be there in the main end of season sale in July next year or even worse New Year, the following year.

Collections tagged, sized and merchandised to

guidelines now take pride of place on the shop floor, positioned in collection order as they build up the look for the season, with the latest at the entrance, just to tempt you and remind you that little black dress has now arrived as you pass en route to the bank on pay day the same week. We are quite the temptress and cunning in our ways. Working the floor now really comes into play.

Working the floor with corns and calluses

"Oh if only I knew then what I know now!" A saying that springs to mind as I begin this chapter. Clarks shoes were a blessing in those early days, cutting my teeth on the shop floor. However, working for a high end brand demanded a change in footwear to finish and complete the polished look and it would come as no surprise to me if others reading this grimace, as they look down to their own feet. This industry certainly leaves its scars in the form of the odd corn and callus. I had been offered a job for my favourite brand. Slim fit – okay, tight fit! – didn't exactly look the part with a walking shoe. No, the boots with 75% staff discount, complete with a 4" heel became the norm, and gradually over time a little reminder of such is now on the second toe in on my left foot. Little corn has become the bane of my life and no amount of corn patches will permanently shift it.

So, what is working the floor? Well, imagine a stage but replace the props with rails and hangers and the actors with sales assistants and there you have it. You weave your way amongst customers and tell the story of the collections. It is an art. Your own personality comes into play. Confidence in yourself and how you develop 'your look' the way you customise the collections to your own style draws ladies to you on the floor, and you work it, not only during opening hours on the floor but also on your way into work. Countless times I am asked at school gates, in the coffee shop or even when I pass through the competition's floor on my way to the bank. Ladies will stop or remark later, "Seeing you in that skirt/ shirt/dress was the inspiration for me to buy as it looked so good on you!" That does sound rather big headed but this is business and it's competitive in the world of fashion in particular, so any opportunity to market the brand you work for should be grabbed with both hands and do so – just work it, girls! Working the floor is what I love and am passionate about in this business and every clever saleswoman out there worth her salt knows how to do it. You simply inspire and have the customer purring for more.

Meet and greet is where it all starts. It is so easy to break the ice – a quick mention of the weather is usually all it takes to start building rapport. I have welcomed in customers as they resemble drowned rats with "Come in, ladies, it's raining; have a browse and dry out whilst it passes – we've an offer on to put the smile back on your face". It usually merits a smile at least, as umbrellas are left for me to guard. Their eyes light up as the top featured in last Sunday's supplement of the Mail is now in sight, and the must-have, as you are wearing it! Flip it round to "Come in, it's hot and we've got

the air-con on" – carries the same weight come the
summer months. They are hot and glowing as yet
again the weathermen got it wrong. Have they ever
had it right since the 1987 Hurricane? My heart
goes out to sales girls in both seasons. I mean, take
a typical February each year, spring collections
being promoted and these poor girls are welcoming
you dressed in such with a warm greeting for you to
enter, browse and purchase. They know there is no
way you are going anywhere near the fitting room
to take off the four layers to try on that cute top you
have eyed for the last few days since you passed by
on your way home – as it is -3 degrees. The fact that
the poor sales girl is wearing it at the entrance to
greet you, and has gone blue with cold, has nothing
to do with it! Get an Indian summer in September
when staff are now promoting winter season – trust
me, if you are glowing she is cooking like a chicken
on gas mark 5!

The stories I could tell from meet and greet and
the laughter had over the years are priceless, but
the one that takes the biscuit has to be the pigeon
and it certainly added some drama to the day.
Having just given directions to a tourist (another
role added to meet and greet – you become a tourist
guide for the city for every nationality going), a
pigeon, quite cheeky in his walk, edged towards
the open doors. Head bobbing from side to side in
perfect timing to his strut he just came in as bold

as brass! I stood in disbelief as he kept on going. Surely, he would turn round having realised the error of his ways and that would be the end of it. Oh no, pigeon was determined. At this point everyone stopped – staff and customers – he had the floor. Staff eyed customers and vice versa. Pigeon just carried on, took a right turn past me, strutted on and settled in the window without so much as a by-your leave, thank you very much. At this point you can imagine what is going through my head – one false move towards pigeon and there will be flapping and a take off with a display worthy of a Red Arrow, not to mention the prospect of a claim from any customer who got in his way. Scenes from Hitchcock's film 'The Birds' were also up there in my thoughts. As luck would have it that day a customer came forward to assist. As much as I am an animal lover, negotiating with a pigeon or any other bird for that matter is not a skill I possess, and pigeon was now having second thoughts about staying. "I have experience handling birds," she said. "Be my guest," I replied. "Thank god" is what actually went through my head at the time! I marched down the floor to get a dust sheet or anything to get operations under way, as speed was now the order of the day. Dust sheet at the ready, minutes later pigeon now dazed as he had decided to try and fly out through the front glass window a couple of times, was captured and gently placed outside the door. It became the talking point on the floor and the ice breaker that day.

By the way, and whilst on the subject of working
the floor, take a moment or two next time you enter
a store on the high street and note the tempo of the
music. Nice and easy, early doors, ladies to soothe
that head from the extra glass of red you had last
night. Yet come service window and up goes the
tempo to match your mood at lunchtime, bright eyed
and bushy tailed ready to shop till you drop as we
floorwalk you round the collections, collecting pieces
and now stepping in time to the music, you head
towards the Fitting Room.

The Fitting Room, Pinafores and Prayer Mat

The chapter I have looked forward to the most and the main reason and motivation for writing my story.

Working the floor with customers leads many of you to the fitting room, some of you with just one item, others with an armful along with a handover from staff which then becomes ammunition to either kill or secure sales. It really is in our hands and not the customers as they think. The fitting room is the hub for all that is to come and memories flood back to me now as I take a sip of tea and look back on them. Even before you enter fitting I will have seen you walking around either on your own or accompanied by an assistant on a floor walk. You have been welcomed in and as you pass by we note your body shape, and are ready to work with you. There is no greater pleasure as a stylist to see a woman of any age and size leave fitting with a piece from a collection for an important occasion knowing she looks amazing. She oozes with an air of self-confidence. Be honest, take your time and she will come back for more. Lie for the sake of a quick sale and she will either return and bury you or simply avoid the brand like the plague, and so will her circle.

Once the curtain is drawn, we wait for it to be flung back with either a swift motion or a soft glide, both actions speak volumes and determine your mood and that's when we get to work with you, chance permitting. The classic line "Does my bum look big in this?" is one I dread, as is "If only I could get rid of this!" as hands move around the hips or the tummy. Then they look you up and down and say "It's okay for you!" – little do they know the divorce diet, being a single mother and on my feet all day is the explanation for my size so let's leave the sarcasm at that and work together. The look we can create might not be the one you envisaged as you came in. As you are busy taking layers off, we will be back out on the floor, returning with alternatives to take you out of the comfort zone you have been in for decades. It is not easy to tell women of any age that pleats will add inches here and there. A simple change of neckline can balance a bust line better than any scalpel or chicken fillet stuffed into a 32A. Your facial expressions speak volumes as you stare at your reflection in the mirror, some with a smile, others with concern and a vow that come Monday morning it's back to the 5-2 diet, cabbage soup, Atkins or any current trendy solution as you only have a month to shift it before the wedding. You are going to get into the dress come hell or high water.

Fitting room mirrors can cause quite a stir, as can lighting, and let us not forget your make-up isn't right, your hair looks like you have been dragged through a hedge backwards, and if that isn't enough you put the wrong knickers on this morning. We say it before you do just to make you feel at ease and reassure you we have seen it countless times before. After all, everyone needs to get home and try it on again in their own environment, with tights instead of socks and with the hope that the jacket, shoes and bag do justice to the dress that's just cost you more than this month's mortgage. To cap it all, when you do get home did you really look like that in the fitting room as you now look like you have put a stone on? Mirror, mirror on the wall comes to mind and I do wish all brands would stop installing fairground glass to fool us all that we can get away with wearing anything that is floral.

A collection a couple of seasons ago involving the humble pinafore dress caused a sensation in fitting. Staff certainly played their part as all shapes and sizes modelled it on the floor and it became the must-have dress for winter. One freezing Friday, one colour combination went in – not just one lady, no, six to be precise. Curtains swung back and forth and sizes passed between all of you who had never met each other before. Discussions between you on roll necks and shirts to be worn underneath, to opaque tights, jackets and knee boots and how times have changed since Twiggy! All that was missing that day was a bottle and we would have had a party in there worth remembering as laughter spilled out and echoed over the entire floor – so infectious everyone else outside the confines of fitting wanted to know the cause of the hilarity. Needless to say 'pinafore' sold out, was replenished only to sell out again and was the bestseller in one colourway. I wonder if Colin survived that day? Let me explain. Women shop in one or two ways – either with or without a man in tow, and if you do decide to shop with your leading man, ladies, we certainly know when he has had enough. If the price tag compared to the price of a pint is anything to go by, added to the fact he has been dragged round every shop since this morning isn't bad enough, kick off for the match is at three – the vital game to determine promotion or relegation this season. The sight of a chair or sofa opposite fitting is a blessing in disguise. He can cool off as he resembles a packhorse going by the number of bags you have left him with, whilst you try on.

Opposite fitting that day sat Colin, and his chatty lady breezed past me into fitting with an armful of dresses. Colin was joined by another gentleman and together they struck up quite a conversation. Talk turned to sport and that was it, between them we had football focus and you could have dropped the bomb. They didn't draw breath for what they could do to the current England manager – and half the squad, come to think of it. Colin's lady passed me, a nod of approval between the two of us had the sale secured and she now wanted the same from her significant other. She stood at the entrance of fitting. "Colin," she whispered – no response. Talk had now moved on to the best local bar as a pint was promised three shops back. "Colin," the voice now pitched higher in the hope of some recognition that she was stood there – nothing. "Colin!" now with the full force of a sergeant major on the parade ground, and yes his ears pricked up. "What do you think?" she said. Without even turning fully round to appreciate the vision in front of him, "Yes fine" came the response and he carried on the conversation with new sofa buddy. The facial expression of delight from vision of glamour was now replaced with hell hath no fury and the words "I'll take the lot!". Well, my dear Colin, you may have the meal deal in the bags of shopping at your feet now as you sit in comfort putting the world to rights, but pick a wall for when you do get home this evening as that is where it is going to land when she has cooked it. She emerged with the 'wait till I get you out of here' look you now recognise and subsequently frog marched him under no uncertain terms to the desk for payment and it was going to be on his flexible card not hers.

Around that time we had a new starter, Jill. I admired her for her laid back approach on the floor; nothing fazed her and to this day nothing really does – she just gets on with it, yet seems to draw anything unusual in the way of customers to her in the process. One Saturday was priceless and proved no exception to the rule of Jill. You just know when a certain look comes across the floor that something is afoot. Shaking my head from side to side with a smile back as if to say "Go on then" she recalled how she had been approached by a lady going into fitting with a dress and tucked under her arm, her mat. Nothing wrong so far. "Can I pray?" was the question. "How long are you going to be?" replied Jill, grateful this happened early on and the fitting room not yet in full swing. "It should be okay," she said but now wanted reassurance that her decision had been the right one. "Let it go." It was agreed for obvious reasons and I do not need to tell you, the reader, why. Within ten minutes and with a relieved Jill, customer had emerged with dress and mat, with the parting shot "I forgot to pray". She added a scarf en route to the cash desk to complete the look and that was that. But it does beg the question when you think about it – to serve or not to serve, and that is a whole new ball game.

To Serve or not to Serve?

Childhood memories of a famous comedy series, together with the frustrations and hilarious encounters faced by staff at the till point come to mind.

There are times when I think modern day episodes are played out daily on the floor, that would surpass the fictional life portrayed by those characters and give the writers a run for their money. The words "Are you free?" have been said more than once with smiles of recognition from customers who know exactly what staff refer to with this one familiar line, remembered in all its glory some 30 years later.

There is a great saying: "Treat others as you would like to be treated". One of the lessons of life I was taught at an early age. How sad that it seems to have been forgotten by many customers when it comes to service. If there is to be any backlash at all from my memoirs this is where it will stem from. But, before the knives are sharpened and you take aim and fire, can you see service from our point of view? Your views are, after all, voiced in no uncertain terms on a daily basis with the knowledge that in your eyes, the minute we open our mouths to defend the manner in which you have spoken to us, the P45 is more or less in the post – as you, the customer are always right. Or are you?

It often intrigues me how customers arrive on the
floor as if possessed by the devil. Body language
often gives you away on your entry, not to mention
your facial expression, a clear indication that battle
is to commence. Personally, I think 'get it out of your
system'. When you have stopped ranting and raving
at me that the "zip gave way halfway through the
most important meeting in your career", or, "the
button just fell off on the first time of wearing", not
forgetting the ever classic "the colour ran in the
wash" – despite the fact the care label states oh so
clearly 'dry clean'! Only then, can we find a solution
under the returns policy. Sadly, we have no control
over courier service delivery standards. You were
promised delivery within 24 hours. That meant
you had to stay in all day and wait for it, glued to
daytime television, tackled your mountain of ironing,
only for them not to turn up between 9 and 6, with
your much awaited and prized juice extractor. To add
insult to injury, you had bought all the vegetables in
the entire aisle of the supermarket in preparation for
the 7 day 7lb loss diet featured in the national daily
paper! Without wishing to dig my grave any deeper,
the fact you had a blazing row with your other half
before you came in this morning has now raised
your blood to boiling point and the first poor sod you
meet on the floor is in for it. Yet to draw breath I
stand and wonder if you saw the news bulletin this
morning of a plane going down and all lives lost. Yet,
here I am, taking full venom for something beyond

my control. Finally, red in the face and breathless you look me full on for an explanation and dare I say retaliation? Sadly, my dear, you will not get it, not for the threat of the P45 in the post, but for the six customers stood behind you at the desk, who would like to say it for me, going by their raised eyebrows. Younger, inexperienced assistants have been seen to dissolve in tears and flee from the floor at this point and you are triumphant in your accomplishment. I have no doubt half your time this evening will be spent recalling the tale to all and sundry on the phone. BT profits will be up this week. However, silence speaks volumes. Have you gone too far? Once your blood pressure has returned to normal you realise that just perhaps you have gone a little overboard. It finally dawns on you that the person in front of you is actually a human being. Your delivery of "I know it's not your fault" comes into play. Usual pleasantries now open up lines of communication between customer and staff with the hope of a solution we can all live with. Amen.

Language barriers can present issues on service. It seems that one country arrives in force on the high street, resembling the arrivals terminal at Heathrow given the numbers and footfall regularly seen. One week the Italians are everywhere; they are then followed by the Chinese, cameras out snapping everything in sight. We had a call from a bus driver to warn us the Russians were coming and sure enough they did, all 12 of them, not the multitude we anticipated going by the conversation earlier. They came, they went and the pile of clothes in fitting, dumped on the floor, evidence of their opinion on current collections. One particular nationality's way of a polite introduction, after you nod out of respect on meet and greet is a pointed finger in your face! Well, good morning to you too! A return of "YES" in a tone of voice back to match pointed index finger of right hand in front of me, but coupled with a fixed smile indicates my displeasure at being summonsed to give service. Not wanting to disrupt foreign relations here, but could you at least master enough English to acknowledge us with "Hello" or "Good Morning", without the need for a translator in attendance?

Disputes at the till point of sale are another bone of contention, particularly in sale. Now, I grew up and learnt my times tables at an early age, without the need for a calculator. I know how to deduct 30% from £15, and it shouldn't need me to tell you the answer. Why you demand I do it for you to determine whether you feel the discount now justifies the purchase beggars belief-and it isn't just one age bracket, it is across the board! One particular customer suggested she was right with her calculations despite the till reading. Proved wrong by the green numbers in front of her she was blushing ever so slightly as I carried on wrapping the mug in several sheets of crepe paper

"Leave it"! she snapped. "It's only going to my office."
That rather legal pitch of voice. And when you do
unwrap it, I thought in my head, take out your school
books from year 5 Maths and learn your ten times
table.

The gist of this chapter is to remind you that like
any other industry, we will, after years of training
modules thrown at us and qualifications gained
to prove we can absorb all that is relevant to be
competent in what we do, try and give you the best
service we can to ensure you enjoy your shopping
experience. Could you at least play your part too in
the relationship between customer and staff?

On the subject of service, the register icon has now
completely disappeared off the screen!

Tills, Technology and "Houston, we have a problem"

With the register now off and facing a blank screen this is the moment I hate. I will be totally honest with you and hold my hands up as I will look for the younger members of staff on the floor. Youth of today has the advantage of growing up with all that is technical. I, on the other hand, came in to it in my twenties and still don't see eye to eye with it! Put me in a kitchen with a recipe, oven and an hour and I can knock up the best cupcakes going. Faced now with a blank screen it is a completely different kettle of fish. No matter which option I tried to revive it, "the computer said no", to coin a famous phrase. Added to the fact that the card pad to take payments from your flexible friend has also joined in meant war was truly now declared between retail assistant and technology – "Houston we have a problem"!

Let's face it when computers are on form they are amazing pieces of machinery, that embrace modern society. When not working, they are the biggest pain going and the queue at the point of sale is now growing. Usually guaranteed to happen most Bank Holiday weekends when stores are crammed with day trippers, eager for a bargain to offset the shock cost of the school uniform before their little darlings return, after the never ending summer holidays.

You are just about to ring through a sale to seal this week's target and without warning the till and all that is technical will shut down. No amount of threats to cut its plugs off or a quick thump to remind it who is the boss here will give you a green light to confirm a blip is over, and normal service resumed. At this point out will come the old manual swipe machines. Remember them? You placed a four layered wad of pre-printed sales receipts into the set area, the customer's plastic charge/debit/ credit card underneath, pulled over the swipe arm and hey presto, you were done. All you needed was the customer's signature to complete. Every brand has one just in case, and it causes quite a stir when brought out of retirement. It wasn't just the music that was great in the eighties: life was simple. Nowadays, technology rules every aspect of our lives-from ordering your weekly shop to annual holidays; you can even set your central heating to come on via text message to your home to ensure you are as snug as a bug in a rug for when you arrive home on the coldest winter's day.

Scanners and printers at sale time test your patience. You switch on and for five minutes you are moving at the speed of light-then nothing! You reboot, it downloads the updates and you are back to normal. Then it changes its mind for security reasons because you didn't log back in within the time limits. When you go through it all again

rebooting, downloading, all within the time allowed,
it then decides it wants to be recharged.
The simplest email poses a problem. You compose,
sign off with regards etc, press the reply to sender
option, only for a box to appear to tell you the
address is not recognised! Well it was at 8.30 am, so
what's the issue now? You try again – not accepted
and on the third attempt you're now blocked. Several
telephone calls later you discover that you missed
a dot off the end of the address that upset little
laptop. When it does decide to play ball with you up
pops a new message in your inbox. You now have
a reminder that the recipient is still awaiting a
response and the deadline was midday.

My own frustrations come into play between me and
the self-service tills at a certain food hall on the
high street. I may whizz round the fresh fruit and
vegetable section faster than Usain Bolt – that is
until it comes to weighing and paying. Ladies, am I
the only one, despite attempting to scan the barcode
every which way but loose, to trigger a curt "please
wait for assistance", which is voiced as a stark
reminder that I have upset the register in front of
me? Yes, I did place my handbag in the correct area,
weighed the fruit after tapping the screen endless
times to find it. I placed it in the bagging area, and, I
might add in the bag provided by you. I am grateful I
know the staff in the food hall. I should, going by the
amount I have spent in there, lured in by the husky

voice of a certain actress on prime time television
adverts over the years, especially at Christmas.
My own addiction to a certain pink pig confection
has nothing to do with it of course! Laughter and
shaking of heads, access codes entered by staff
silence the irritating voice. I know full well that I
will go through the whole procedure again on my
next visit, as will the other four stood in line with
the same issue. Perhaps it is time to dispense with
self-service and rely on conveyor belts. We all know
where we stand with this system. At least there
is the friendly banter with the checkout assistant
to ease the shock of the cost of bananas, kiwi and
broccoli. The hamster will be happy this evening,
which is more than can be said for my little one at
the sight of green florets, guaranteed to initiate a
stand-off at the dinner table at any time.

The Staff Room

The one room, where staff can unload and voice their opinions without the threat of any repercussions.

Off the floor and off with the shoes for the designated time on your shift where caffeine, papers, mobile phones and Kindles are the norm.

The highs and lows of retail with laughter and tears and volumes of sound bouncing off the wall as encounters on the floor during the day are recalled between staff members on breaks, each with their own tales to tell. The same walls are covered with familiar target charts and figures keeping us all on our toes for the week ahead. Thank-you cards and notes to remind us of a job well done. Goodbye cards from staff long gone serve as a reminder of the turnover of staff this business is renowned for. A table is littered with the latest glossies, each with its own view on the trends ahead that will be the look for the coming season and will be soon flooding the high street; and stick thin models airbrushed to look perfect, who, given the opportunity, would gladly tuck into the holiday sweets, biscuits and birthday cake left for us all to sample.

Topics of conversation are no different to any other staff room up and down the country. Last night's storyline in the soaps is always a favourite along with Strictly Come Dancing or any other seasonal favourite. Daily horoscopes will be read out – the promise that it really could be you to win the lottery, Aries, if you use lucky number 8. A quirky conversation over the scene from a film where a dear friend dies close to the sea in a deckchair prompted several suggestions of location in the UK, together with choices of rug from the stockroom! It had me humming 'wind beneath my wings' for the remainder of the day.

Do any of us really care that there is no milk in the fridge again? Or that the unclaimed cheese sandwich sat on the middle shelf, now looking sad for itself and four days past its sell-by date and growing bacteria nicely, thank you very much? Endless bottles of chilled water can be found regularly lined up to offset the dehydrating effects of the shop floor, or, more to the point, last night's staff get together, when we all put the world to rights. We all said we would be sensible ,it being a school night, only to abandon that ruling on the second glass of Pimms on a glorious summer's evening. And yes we do voice our opinions and recall the morning's events and what we would really like to say to the wonderful customer, who told us in no uncertain terms what we could do with a shift dress... crumpled and now waiting for the security tag to be reapplied, placed on a hanger to standard and put back out onto the floor to be resold. Your sheepish look gave you away

and yes you may have returned said dress within 28
days for a refund, but we know you have worn it. The
price tag you insist is missing may well be missing
but the aroma of Chanel no 5 is not – yet this has no
bearing in your eyes!

Dramas and dreams all live in this room, as does the
clock as a reminder to wash your mug and return
to the floor, ready for the next instalment of the
working day.

Conclusion

This is where I take my leave. I thought of ending with "What is a retail assistant?", but there is little point. The chapters speak volumes. Never underestimate us or the qualities we possess, or feel you have the right to dismiss us as unworthy of respect or value. Just meet us halfway sometimes, preferably with a smile. It's not too much to ask and free of charge.

COMING SOON

'Shopgirl Secrets from the High Street'